I0813150

An Imprint of Pop!
popbooksonline.com

American Indians

THE SIOUX

by N.C. Barnes

WELCOME TO DiscoverRoo!

This book is filled with videos, puzzles, games, and more! Scan the QR codes* while you read, or visit the website below to make this book pop.

popbooksonline.com/Sioux

abdobooks.com

Published by Pop!, a division of ABDO, PO Box 398166, Minneapolis, Minnesota 55439.

Printed in the United States of America, North Mankato, Minnesota.

052024
082024

THIS BOOK CONTAINS RECYCLED MATERIALS

Cover Photo: Shiiko Alexander/Alamy Stock Photo
Interior Photos: Getty Images, Shutterstock Images, Wikimedia
Editor: Emily Dreher
Series Designer: Colleen McLaren

Library of Congress Control Number: 2023947499

Publisher's Cataloging-in-Publication Data

Names: Barnes, N.C., author.
Title: The Sioux / by N.C. Barnes
Description: Minneapolis, Minnesota : Pop!, 2025 | Series: American Indians | Includes online resources and index
Identifiers: ISBN 9781098246235 (lib. bdg.) | ISBN 9781098246792 (ebook)
Subjects: LCSH: Lakota Indians--Juvenile literature. | American Indians--Juvenile literature. | Indians of North America--Juvenile literature. | Indigenous peoples--Social life and customs--Juvenile literature. | Cultural anthropology--Juvenile literature.
Classification: DDC 973.0497--dc23

*Scanning QR codes requires a web-enabled smart device with a QR code reader app and a camera.

TABLE OF CONTENTS

CHAPTER 1

WHO ARE THE SIOUX?

Before European **settlers** came to North America, the land was mostly wild and open. It was populated by American Indians. Each group had its own languages and culture. Culture is the customs, arts, and ideas of a group of people.

WATCH A VIDEO HERE!

The Sioux people valued being good family members.

Dogs helped the Sioux people travel.

The Great Sioux Nation includes the Dakota, Nakota, and Lakota peoples. They call themselves *Oceti Sakowin,* meaning "Seven Council Fires."

The Seven Council Fires refers to the seven original bands of the Sioux Nation.

The three groups began far apart, but eventually, they all lived on the plains of North America. The Sioux are one of the oldest American Indian nations. Their history dates back 3,000 years.

Each Sioux village had one chief.

The Sioux are **nomadic** people of the Great Plains. Historically, their territory covered land in modern day Minnesota, North Dakota, South Dakota, Montana, Wyoming, Colorado, and Nebraska. The seven Sioux subnations are made of bands called *ospaye*. Bands included several families with common **ancestors**. These family groups were called *tiospaye*.

Sioux homeland had beautiful rock formations.

SIOUX HOMELANDS

CANADA

MONTANA

NORTH DAKOTA

MINNESOTA

SOUTH DAKOTA

WYOMING

NEBRASKA

COLORADO

HISTORICAL SIOUX TERRITORY

The Sioux lived in specific parts of the highlighted area.

Bands made decisions together during council fires.

Oceti Sakowin people were led by older women in the ospaye. Leaders were chosen by other members based on wisdom and love they had shown for their traditions and people. They didn't tell other members what to do. Instead they gave suggestions and guidance.

SACRED BLACK HILLS

Oceti Sakowin call the Black Hills *He Sapa.* They are **sacred** to the Sioux. The land holds their memories and stories. Legend says a group of girls were playing in the Black Hills. They became surrounded by hungry bears. A voice from the sky told them to climb a hill. Once they were on the hill, it rose high in the air. The girls were saved from the bears. The raised landform still exists. It is called *Mato Tipila.*

Mato Tipila is located in Wyoming.

CHAPTER 2

HISTORICAL LIFE

The Sioux followed bison herds around the plains. Millions of wild bison once roamed the Sioux's homeland. Oceti Sakowin were hunters and gatherers. They hunted bison, deer, and turkeys. They gathered fruits, vegetables, and grains from the land. They traded with other tribes for corn.

LEARN MORE HERE!

Bison were sacred animals to the Sioux because of all they could provide.

Hunting bison was important to the Oceti Sakowin. Men waited to start a hunt until a **spiritual** leader had a vision about where to go. Then a council discussed and planned the hunt carefully. The whole village moved where the council chose to hunt.

The Oceti Sakowin were expert bison hunters even before they had horses.

Bison meat was dried so it would stay good to eat for a long time.

The Sioux used every part of the bison. They used the meat for food and the skin for clothes, blankets, and homes. They used the bones for tools, needles, and utensils. The Oceti Sakowin traded goods made from bison.

Tepees were shaped to remain standing during strong winds.

The people of the Great Sioux Nation lived in tepees. Tepees were made from pine poles tied at the top and spread in a circle at the bottom. The frame was wrapped with bison hides. It had a hole at the top to release smoke from the fire kept inside. When it was time for bands to move, they used the poles to carry their things. The poles were tied to horses for travel.

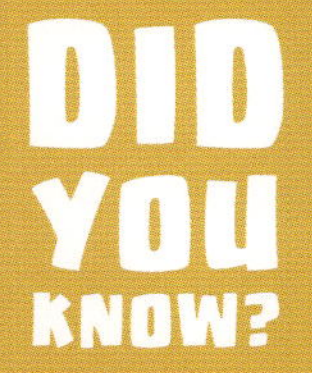

Before the Sioux people had horses, they used dogs to drag goods while they traveled. Tepees were smaller then.

All clothing worn by Sioux people was made from animal skin. Men wore shirts, **breechcloths**, and leggings. Women wore leggings and shirts that were often decorated with fringe. Sioux wore moccasins that were waterproof. In the winter, moccasins were lined with fur. Bison furs were used as winter robes and blankets.

Some Sioux wore decorated bison robes for important ceremonies.

CHAPTER 3

FAMILY AND TRADITIONS

The Sioux people were connected through their mothers. When couples got married, they lived with the woman's band. **Kinship** is very important to the Sioux. They also value their connection with all of creation.

EXPLORE LINKS HERE!

Women cared for the home, cooked, and gathered. They set up and took down tepees when it was time to move. They also prepared bison hides and sewed clothes for the members of the band. Men hunted food, protected the band, and traded with neighbors. Men earned respect for brave deeds performed during hunts or battles.

Children called the older women and men of their tiospaye mother and father.

Children were raised and cared for by everyone in their village. They lived near cousins and grandparents, so they could play all the time. Children were taught to be very quiet. They couldn't startle the bison herds.

Children in villages referred to each other as brother, sister, or cousin.

A large community tepee was at the center of Sioux villages.

When boys turned 12, they started living with older, unmarried men from their band. They learned how to hunt, protect their people, and other things men needed to know. Girls stayed with their parents until they married. They learned skills from other women in their family.

DID YOU KNOW?

The Sioux traded with Europeans and other American Indian tribes.

Paint was made from plants, dirt, and animal parts.

The Oceti Sakowin believe that all life came from the Creator. All life is connected through Mother Earth, and there is a natural balance to things. **Spiritual** leaders performed **ceremonies** during important times of the year. They also healed people.

The Sioux were artists. They decorated their clothes and moccasins in beautiful patterns made from porcupine quills and beads. They painted their tepees with images of nature and important historical events. They are best known for their winter count.

Oceti Sakowin painted bison hides.

DID YOU KNOW? Winter counts kept track of time and important events. Every winter, an image was added to a hide to represent the year.

CHAPTER 4

FIGHTING FOR THEIR HOMELAND

White **settlers** began moving west of the Mississippi River in the 1800s. The Sioux people had to protect their homeland from being invaded. They fought on horseback with bows and arrows. Eventually, they fought with guns.

COMPLETE AN ACTIVITY HERE!

Sioux were skilled at horseback riding.

White settlers did not respect the Sioux's land. They hunted bison to near **extinction**. The US Army warred with the Oceti Sakowin for decades. The Sioux lost their final fight at Wounded Knee Creek in 1890.

In 1973, American Indians took over Wounded Knee for 71 days. They wanted more control of their homeland.

The Sioux people brought their culture and traditions to their reservations.

The US government forced the remaining bands of Sioux from their homeland and onto **reservations**. At first, the US government let the Sioux keep the Black Hills, but soon settlers stole that land too.

Today, the Sioux live on reservations in North Dakota, South Dakota, Nebraska, Minnesota, and Canada. Life can be hard on the reservations. But Oceti Sakowin are

In 2017, the Standing Rock Sioux Tribe marched to protect water on their land.

strong people, and they celebrate their history and traditions. They hope one day see their **sacred** Black Hills returned to them.

MAKING CONNECTIONS

TEXT-TO-SELF

Family is very important to the Sioux people. Children are raised by their extended families. Would you like to have been raised that way? What do you think would be the best or worst part?

TEXT-TO-TEXT

Have you read about another American Indian nation? How is their culture similar to or different from the Sioux people?

TEXT-TO-WORLD

American settlers were responsible for the near extinction of the Sioux people's sacred animal, the bison. What are some other animals that have nearly gone extinct? How can humans help them survive?

GLOSSARY

ancestor — a person from whom one is descended.

breechcloth — a cloth worn over the groin.

ceremony — a formal event held on a special occasion.

extinction — the condition of no longer existing.

kinship — the quality or state of being related.

nomadic — relating to people who travel from place to place.

reservation — a piece of land set aside by the government for American Indians to live on.

sacred — something worthy of intense honor.

settler — a person who moves with a group of others to live in a new country or area. A place where settlers live is called a settlement.

spiritual — having to do with people's beliefs in things, such as the soul, nature, and what happens after death.

INDEX

DiscoverRoo!
ONLINE RESOURCES

This book is filled with videos, puzzles, games, and more! Scan the QR codes* while you read, or visit the website below to make this book pop.

popbooksonline.com/Sioux

*Scanning QR codes requires a web-enabled smart device with a QR code reader app and a camera.